IN THE SHADOW OF GOD'S MIRACLES
THE LIFE STORY OF MARIE-ROZELLE PAMPHILE

Pittsburgh, Pennsylvania USA

In the Shadow of God's Miracles
by Marie-Rozelle Pamphile
Copyright ©2023 Marie-Rozelle Pamphile

ISBN 978-1-63360-261-8

All rights reserved. This book is protected under the copyright laws of the United States of America. This book may not be copied or reprinted for commercial gain or profit.

Scripture quotations are taken from THE HOLY BIBLE: New International Version ©1978 by the New York International Bible Society, used by permission of Zondervan Bible Publishers. All rights reserved.

For Worldwide Distribution Printed in the U.S.A.

Urban Press
P.O. Box 8881
Pittsburgh, PA 15221-0881
412.646.2780
www.urbanpress.us

"All things are possible with God."
Luke 1:37

"For I know the plans I have
for you, declares the Lord,
plans to prosper you and
not to harm you,
plans to give you hope and a future."
Jeremiah 29:11

This book is dedicated to my beloved husband, Leon, for his support throughout my life and to my children—Rose Ellen, Françoise Martine, and Frantz Marcel—and to their spouses and my grandchildren.

Table of Contents

Introduction — viii

Chapter 1
Haiti, My Country of Birth — 1

Chapter 2
A Peaceful Childhood — 14

Chapter 3
Orphanage Stay — 26

Chapter 4
Coming to America — 35

Chapter 5
Tying the Knot with the Love of My Life — 48

Chapter 6
Walking with Jesus — 56

Chapter 7
Experiencing God's Miracles — 64

Chapter 8
Blessed with a Nice Family — 74

Conclusion — 90

Biography — 92

ACKNOWLEDGEMENTS

I am taking this opportunity to extend a heartfelt gratitude to my family and friends who have made possible the writing of this book. It was at a board meeting of the Functional Literacy Ministry that Kathy Bynum heard a testimony of my life. She persuaded me to write the whole story. Through my conversation with my friend, Inez Miles, she put me in touch with Dr. John Stanko who accepted to undertake the project.

My gratitude also goes to Cathy Sapp, Mary Johnston, and Dr. Barbara Rogers who encouraged me in the past to write the story of my life. I express profound appreciation to my beloved husband, Leon, who was an immense help in drafting the story. Thanks to my daughter, Rose Ellen, who helped with editing and formatting the book. May all who have contributed in the writing of this book find here the full expression of my indebtedness.

Introduction

By Leon D. Pamphile

The book of Genesis relates the amazing story of the creation: the heavens and the earth, the seas and skies, the moon and stars, etc. Genesis also speaks of human beings created in the image of God. From the very beginning, God has also established the relevance and importance of human relationships. The book highlights the relationships between God and nature, between God and man, and between man and man. In this very setting, it has clearly established that man cannot live in isolation.

When God came to the garden of Eden and discovered Adam's loneliness, he readily solved this issue by creating for him a mate in his likeness. The Bible says that God put Adam to sleep and took from his body a rib with which he created the woman. When God brought Eve to Adam, he exclaimed with amazement,

*This is now bone of my bones
and flesh of my flesh* (Genesis 2:23).

I can surely identify with Adam's ecstatic reaction and exultation upon his first encounter with Eve, for the same level of bliss and euphoria attended my soul when I first encountered a beautiful teen-aged girl by the name of Marie Rozelle. God must have surely used one of my ribs to create her just for me for the deep love I initially experienced upon our first meeting has been shining brighter and brighter as we have journeyed together through the years.

There are a thousand and one ways to introduce my Rozelle to you. Let's begin with the person I have known and loved over the last six decades. Rozelle is a short and beautifully-built lady. Through God's grace, she has been enjoying well-being. Rozelle is a child of God who has been dwelling in the shadow of the Lord Almighty. She is blessed with beautiful features which definitely remind me of the lover in the Song of Songs from whom I borrow these lines:

> *How beautiful, my darling*
> *oh, how beautiful.*
> *Your eyes are doves*
> (Song of Songs 1:15).

How well do I identify with this gentleman who sang of his love for his beloved. Rozelle is as beautiful. When away from her, I often dreamed of her attractive countenance and visualized her dazzling smile. When in her presence, I too like a bird never fail to sing to her of how thankful I am that she has lovingly chosen to share with me our life journey.

Rozelle is also blessed with a powerful inner beauty that enables her to display kindness and goodness. She loves people and seeks every opportunity to touch their lives. When we attend church or other social events, I always find myself waiting for her, for she takes time to talk a little longer than I do with others. I praise God to have endowed me with much patience.

Let me confess that I, too, have been the

beneficiary of her kindness. I remember well how worried I was because I did not have the material resources to get married and support a family. Both of us were young and deprived of money. I often thought of this situation which at times caused me many worrisome and anxious moments.

One day, I opened my heart and confessed to her how much I worried about the possibility of ever getting married and being together with her in any foreseeable future. She attentively listened to me. Then she lovingly responded by whispering to my soul encouraging words that were truly a strong and efficacious medicine. She conveyed to me that the Lord had left us a powerful legacy in the Gospel of Matthew: "Don't worry about tomorrow, for tomorrow will worry about itself. Each day has enough trouble of its own" (Matthew 6:34).

I left her that day with a burden lifted from my heart. I felt delivered as I just engaged the path of a worry-free life. The Lord did make a way for us to later get married. It has been over five decades now since we tied the knot and we have been enjoying life through the thick and thin of its vicissitudes.

Rozelle and I have been blessed with a beautiful family of two daughters and one son. We now have five grandsons and an adopted granddaughter. We trained our children in the fear of the Lord and we currently enjoy sharing their lives and the lives of our grandchildren.

Rozelle's life has been such a blessing to others. On this account, it reminds me of the life of Abraham when the Lord called him to embark by faith on a new and adventurous journey. God made Abraham a promise with a sevenfold structure: 1) I will make you into great nation; 2) I will bless you; 3) I will make your name great; 4) you will be a blessing: 5) I will bless those who bless you; 6) whoever curses you, I will curse; and 7) all people on earth will be blessed through you (see Genesis 12: 2). We feel today blessed through Abraham We are his spiritual descendants.

Rozelle is also Abraham's spiritual descendant. Like Abraham, the Lord has miraculously used her to be a blessing to many people in her family circle and beyond. The very first point of this circle was myself. Let me confess that like many Haitians, it was my desire to come and study in the United States in search of a better life. For many years, this quest seemed a complete illusion. I was back then an interpreter who came in contact with many American missionaries. Some of them made promises to send the necessary papers for me to travel to America. These promises had all remained mere broken promises.

God made it that some aspects of the sevenfold structure of the promises made to Abraham became relevant for me through Rozelle. In the second part, the Lord said to Abraham "I will bless you" and in part four, he affirmed "you will be a blessing" (Genesis 12:2). Rozelle was blessed to come first to the United States in 1968. Then one year later, she came back to Haiti to marry me, thus enabling me to make the journey as well. Through her, the circle widened to include siblings from both sides of our families who were also blessed in later years to come to the United States.

Another important dimension of Rozelle's life is being for me a wonderful wife. Proverbs 31 offers a complimentary and insightful picture of the wife and mother who knows how to care for her family. She supports well her husband and helps in the training of the children. For these virtues, she commands respect and honor. The wise man proclaimed that he who finds a good wife has found a treasure that is worth more than jewels, as he explains in clear terms:

Charm is deceitful,
and beauty is vain,
but a woman who
fears the Lord is to be praised
(Proverbs 31:30).

Rozelle is a good provider for the physical and emotional needs of her children. She carried two daughters and one son. She raised them to love the Lord their God and to walk in the path of righteousness. She is a good mother who teaches her children in keeping the divine laws. We give thanks daily for our wonderful family.

Rozelle is also driven to bring service to the needy in the community of Pittsburgh where her influence in doing good is widely known and appreciated. Besides being a good wife who looks to the needs of her own family, she opens her hands to the poor and reaches out her hands to the needy (see Proverbs 31:20): "She opens her mouth with wisdom, and the teaching of kindness is on her tongue" (Proverbs 31:26).

Additionally, I am glad to have her as my

secret weapon as someone once made it clear to me. As such, Rozelle embodies the virtues of a perfect wife, a bishop's wife, shining in that role with exceptional splendor. It was Cynthia Wilkins, a missionary with a special heart for Haiti, who underscored that point to me. Cynthia is a member of the Bethel Cathedral Church of God in Christ in San Francisco, California and was instrumental in having her church send a monthly contribution to Haiti for a few decades now. Her love for Haiti was even more manifest in 2019 when she made a trip to Haiti to attend our national convocation. What a great time she had with the delegation she brought with her in discovering and learning to love a people her church has supported for so many years.

To make it a pleasant time for Cynthia and her two friends, we invited them after the convocation to join us to the mountains where we have our residence. In one of our conversations, she made a statement that remains implanted in my heart. She said, "You know that Lady Rozelle is your secret weapon." What a revealing and encouraging statement! She has been a secret weapon in many ways. She has been more effective than I on many occasions to convince many to support my ministry in the church and the Functional Literacy Ministry of Haiti. The more I think about it, the more I realize the tremendous impact Rozelle has made on my life throughout the years in my various endeavors.

As a sign of appreciation and gratitude, I am delighted to introduce to you someone who has made such a meaningful contribution on my life extending over a period of six decades. She has injected hope in my life. We both have learned to wait on the Lord. It is amazing to realize how with time our patience has handily paid off. It is a manifestation of the power of God's extended hand to us as his beloved children. Again, it is the author of the Song of Songs that translates so well the matchless power of love and its positive impact on human life:

> *Place me like a seal over your arm,*
> *for love is as strong as death,*
> *its jealousy unyielding as the grave.*
> *It burns like blazing fire,*
> *like a mighty flame.*
> *Many waters cannot quench love*
> *rivers cannot wash it away*
> *If one were to give*
> *all the wealth of his house for love*
> *it would be utterly scorned*
> (Song of Songs 8:6-7).

Let me invite you to read this life story of a blessed woman of God. She will share with you how God has brought her through the adversity of life to place her on the path of victory. It is not only a beautiful story but also an inspiring one that will motivate you to hold on to God's unchanging hands in all circumstances of life. My friends, you are about to enjoy and be blessed by the wonderful story of a beautiful woman, a true child of God. It is my expectation and hope that you will be touched and your life will be fully enhanced by her story, wholly filled with God's intervention and grace.

The trajectory of Rozelle's life has surely evolved in the shadows of God's miraculous power. Living in a country like Haiti where the basic necessities of life are not always available requires great faith. It brings to mind the story of Jesus traveling in Gentile territory when a woman approached and begged him to cure her little daughter who was troubled in her mind. Jesus seemed reluctant, arguing that he had come to save Jewish people, not Gentiles. Desperate, the woman argued back. Wouldn't he pity her despite her nationality? If he were eating, wouldn't he throw scraps to the dogs?

This Canaanite woman did not take no for an answer. Jesus, taken aback by her persistence, rewarded her faith by curing her daughter. Her indomitable faith won her a blessing. In fact, Jesus affirmed her saying, "Woman, great is your faith. Let it be done for you as you wish" (Matthew 15:28).

It was a powerful miracle demonstrating the compassion of Jesus for the poor and the destitute. Rozelle had to live every day of her life, and even so during the days of her youth, expecting divine miracles for daily bread, for healing from every sickness and disease, and for satisfaction of all her needs. Like the Canaanite woman, Rozelle had to exercise great faith to survive in a place where everything was lacking. In many difficult situations, she was not discouraged. Like the Canaanite woman, she learned how to pray and saw prayer work for her in many difficult situations.

Walking in the Shadow of God's Miracles tells the story of God's wondrous deeds for a young woman raised in poverty in

Haiti and touched in every way by the unfailing love of God. To fully appreciate Rozelle's story, it is most relevant to know something about the place where we were born and grew up. We will invite some of you to visit and others to revisit succinctly the history of the Republic of Haiti.

>Bishop Leon Pamphile
>Pittsburgh, Pennsylvania USA
>October 2023

Chapter 1

Haiti— Land of My Birth

I have been living all my life in the shadow of God's miracles and I can testify that God has worked marvelous things on my behalf throughout my life. I am living evidence of what God can do to ensure the well-being of his people. You cannot understand well my story unless you get some basic understanding of the environment where I was born, and spent my early years: in the nation of Haiti.

Haiti, my country of birth. is a small island in the West Indies with a very rich history and cultural background. Haitians are traditionally proud of their country for being the first black independent republic in the world. Furthermore, Haiti has the unique distinction of being the first and only country to earn its independence from colonial slavery through armed struggle. Consequently, Haitians are also quite in tune with the leadership role played by our country in the struggle for the liberation of other oppressed people in the Western hemisphere and Africa.

THE COUNTRY AND ITS LANDSCAPE

Haiti covers 10,714 square miles (27,750 kilometers), which is about the size of the state of Maryland. The island, which is the second largest in the Caribbean after Cuba, comprises two countries: the Spanish-speaking Dominican Republic and Haiti.

The original name of the island was AYTI. That name was given it by the aborigines, the indigenous people who inhabited the island before Spanish colonization. The name means "mountainous country" and indeed, three quarters of the Haitian terrains is mountainous. The highest peak is called "Morne la Selle" with a height of 2,680 meters (8,793 feet) above sea level.

Haiti is prone to natural disasters. At the heart of this predicament stands a tectonic fault line which runs through the country, causing occasional and sometimes devastating earthquakes. In 2010, a horrible earthquake destroyed the capital city of Port-au-Prince and the Western department causing an approximate 300,000 deaths. In 2021, another earthquake hit southern Haiti, causing great destruction of properties and loss of lives.

In addition, Haiti is also located in the Caribbean hurricane belt. In September 2008, four hurricanes and tropical storms Fay, Gustav, Hannah, and Ike slammed into the country with devastating force. Nearly 800 people were killed, 300 remain missing and more than 500 were injured. More than 150,000 people were displaced. Cities and towns were inundated with mud.

Haiti has a warm, humid tropical

climate but temperatures are modified by elevation. Average temperatures range from the high 70s F (about 25 °C) in January and February to the mid-80s F (about 30 °C) in July and August. The village of Kenscoff, at an altitude of some 4,700 feet (1,430 meters), has an average temperature of about 60 °F (16 °C), whereas Port-au-Prince at sea level, has an average of 79 °F (26 °C). In winter, frost can occur at higher elevations.

Haiti also stands out by the beauty of its landscape. When the French colonizers settled in the Hispaniola Island, they called it "La Perle des Antilles" (the Pearl of the Antilles) because of its natural beauty. This factor, along with its warm climate, contribute to making it very attractive for tourism, which played an important role in the economy during the '40s and '50s.

Unfortunately, much of the natural vegetation has been destroyed through clearing for agriculture, grazing, and logging. Deforestation greatly accelerated during the 20th century as the population increased, and the forests that once covered the country have been reduced to a tiny proportion of the total land area.

THE PEOPLE OF HAITI

The current population of Haiti is about eleven million inhabitants. About two million live in metropolitan Port-Au-Prince and other large cities, but the majority live in the countryside. This population is predominantly black except for a small percentage of mulattoes who are the product of the relationships between the former white masters and African slave women. The country still bears the cultural features of the different groups that have lived on its soil.

Haiti is known for its rich cultural heritage. The island was the crossroads where different cultural streams merged for several reasons. First, the Indians who were exterminated by the Spaniards left many traces of their past. This is evident in the great number of Indian words that became part of the Haitian language, "the Creole."

Second, their influence is also noticeable in some of their techniques that are still used in the arts of pottery and weaving. Finally, many religious beliefs of the Haitian people are directly inherited from the Indian original background and culture.

As for the French, their contribution to the Haitian culture is considerable. The heritage of the language is particularly important. Since independence, the official language of Haiti has been French. In 1987, the Haitian constitution made Creole (Kreyol) an official language along with French. Kreol is a French-based vernacular language that developed in the late 17th and early 18th centuries. It emerged primarily on the sugarcane plantations of Haiti from contacts between French colonists and African slaves. Kreol is the first language of about 95 percent of Haitians. The impact of the French past is also striking in Haitian manners and artistic forms.

Above all, there is the African heritage. Most Haitians are of African descent. The traditions transplanted from Africa to the islands by the former slaves are more easily perceivable in Haiti today. Haitian culture has its roots in the daily living of the people manifested in their customs, traditions, works, and beliefs. But there are other features that characterize the culture of the nation.

An analysis of the Haitian culture would be incomplete without giving consideration to the artistic life of the people. Literature is one of the leading arts in Haiti. There is a rich production of literary works consisting of poetry, novels, stories, and plays. Haitian literature which began with the independence of the nation has been the instrument of defense and preservation of Haitian culture throughout the history of the country. Besides literature, painting also contributes a great deal to spread Haitian culture in many foreign countries. Haitian works of art are known and appreciated in exhibitions around the world.

At the beginning, painting was usually a matter of individual interest, but its development became more organized with the foundation in 1944 of the "Centre D'Art" (Art Center), which is a school geared to give special education to Haitian artists. A group of painters came out of that institution with some common creative interests. This tendency which appeared in their production is called "Primitivism." The works of those artists are simple, full of details, and very colorful. Their source of inspirations is again the day-to-day activities of the people and the facts of the national folklore.

Besides painting, the art of wood carving is very popular in Haiti. Those artists produce mainly for the tourist market. In Port-Au-Prince, there are many artifact shops, especially for tourists. They offer pieces that are illustrations of local realities representing the heroes of our country, women carrying baskets on their heads, some religious symbols, and so forth.

HISTORY

Haiti was discovered on December 5, 1492, by Christopher Columbus and his fellow Spaniards. Afterwards, they conquered the island on behalf of the Spanish crown. Thus began the period of colonization that lasted for many centuries. At the time of the discovery, the first inhabitants were the Taino-Indians. They were a people with peaceful manners, leading a tranquil life. They made a living from hunting, fishing, and agriculture. But the Spaniards reduced them to slavery by putting them to hard work to exploit the Hispaniola gold mines. Before long, the Indian population was completely decimated. Their extermination opened a new historical chapter for the island. The Spaniards paved the way for importing black people from the African continent to be enslaved in the colonies of the New World.

The slave trade that subsequently emerged in 1503 was greatly expanded by the French who later gained control over the Western part of the island after driving out the Spaniards. By 1789, more than half a million blacks were imported to Saint-Domingue (San Domingo) under French control. They endured the atrocity of slavery until a genial leader named Toussaint L'Overture led them to revolt against the colonial system. What ensued was a bloody revolution which lasted over a decade. Black slaves and free mulattoes united under the leadership of Jean-Jacques Dessalines to defeat the expeditionary forces sent by French Emperor Napoleon Bonaparte. And in the year 1804, Haiti became an independent country, the first black republic of the world and the only colony to have won its independence through armed struggle.

The Haitian revolution was influenced by the previous American revolution of 1776, and the French revolution of 1789. The Haitian revolution has been, however, buried in the backside of history. Yet it was only the Haitian Revolution that extended freedom and human rights to all regardless of race and ethnic background. Haiti under the visionary Toussaint Louverture sought to realize the ideals of the U.S. Declaration of Independence and the French Declaration of the Rights of Man for all men. The Haitian Revolution thus overcame the contradictions of the American Revolution and the French Revolution because both the United States and France were still colonial powers harboring slavery.

The new nation was, however, ostracized by the colonial powers of the times: France, Spain, England and of course the United States. They led a campaign of denigration of Haiti and built around it a sanitary belt to prevent any form of exportation of the revolution. At the request of France, President Thomas Jefferson sent a bill to Congress prohibiting trade with Haiti. In addition to this embargo, the United categorically refused to recognize Haiti's independence. This exclusion lasted until after the Civil War when President Abraham Lincoln finally recognized Haiti claiming he saw "no good reason" why the United States should "persevere longer in withholding our recognition of the independence and sovereignty of this Caribbean neighbor."

In the course of the nineteenth century, Haiti went through a long period of sociopolitical instability. Two years after the independence, its new leader and founding father, Jean-Jacques Dessalines, was assassinated. Chronic revolutions and civil wars were common through the years. That situation gave a good pretext to President Woodrow Wilson to order American Marines to occupy the country from 1915 until 1934. For decades after that, the political and social conditions have been relatively stable.

During the twentieth century, however, Haiti fell prey to an autocratic dictatorship. In 1957, François (Papa Doc) Duvalier ascended to the presidency following a violent electoral campaign. For fourteen long years, Papa Doc ruled with an iron fist. The country fell into systematic human rights violations. Before he died, the dictator changed the constitution so he could be succeeded by his son, Jean-Claude. Both father and sons maintained power for about three decades, protected by a fierce militia known as "Tonton Macoutes," later labeled "Volontaires de la Sécurité Nationale" (VSN). Both ruled ruthlessly, crushing all human-rights values.

Overwhelmed by two months of violent anti-government protests, Jean-Claude Duvalier resigned the presidency on February 7, 1986. He boarded a U.S. Air Force plane bound for France, ending 28 years of family rule in Haiti. With his departure, Haiti returned to the instability reminiscent of the period prior to the U.S. Marine intervention in 1915. A new constitution was approved by a national referendum. An election was finally organized by the Haitian Supreme Court Judge, Ertha Pascale Trouillot. The presidential election, held on December 16, 1990, resulted in victory for Jean-Bertrand Aristide, a former Salesian order priest.

Aristide gained prominence through his inflammatory sermons against Jean-Claude "Baby Doc" Duvalier. His government was, however, short-lived. The army deposed the new president after only eight months in office. On September 29, 1991, Lt. General Raoul Cédras commanded the bloody coup against Aristide, arresting him and forcing him into exile in Venezuela.

For some two years, the United States, the Organization of American States, and the United Nations led intense negotiations to restore Aristide to power. Despite various embargoes imposed on the country by these international organizations, the Cédras junta resisted any negotiated solution. On September 10, 1994, President Bill Clinton authorized the invasion of Haiti with the military force called "Operation Uphold Democracy." About 20,000 troops, soldiers of the 82nd Airborne, Marines on ships off Haiti, and commandos conducted the assault that dislodged the military junta from power.

Today's Haiti is still mired in political instability and violence. Poverty remains massive and deep, and economic disparity is wide. The country's economic problems worsened when, on January 12, 2010, a 7.0-magnitude earthquake struck Haiti. The devastation was incredible: It left the capital city Port-au-Prince devastated. About 300,000 people were reportedly killed. The government of Haiti estimated that 250,000 residences and 30,000 commercial buildings collapsed or were severely damaged.

Haiti's challenge to provide for the welfare of its people remains huge. While it had not yet recovered from the 2010 disaster, it was struck by another earthquake in the summer of 2021 which devastated the southern peninsula. Haiti's economic and social development continues to be hindered by political instability, increasing violence, and unprecedented level of insecurity. Economic recovery is also stalled by a highly polarized political climate. On July 7, 2021 at 1 a.m., President Jovenel Moïse was assassinated at his residence by a group of 28 foreign mercenaries.

SOCIO-ECONOMIC ISSUES

Data from the World Bank indicates that Haiti remains the poorest country in the Latin American and Caribbean region (LAC) and among the poorest countries in the world. In 2021, Haiti had a GDP per capita of US $1,815, the lowest in the LAC region and less than a fifth of the LAC average of $15,092. On the United Nations' Human Development Index, Haiti ranked 170 out of 189 countries in 2020.

According to the Human Capital Index, children born today in Haiti will grow up to be only 45 percent as productive as they could be if they had enjoyed full access to quality education and healthcare. Over one-fifth of children are at risk of cognitive and physical limitations, and only 78 percent of 15-year-olds will survive to age 60. In light of these figures, let us focus on three key areas related to the state of poverty in Haiti: education, health care, and welfare.

EDUCATION

Education is officially compulsory for children between the ages of 6 and 12. However, because of a lack of facilities and staff, a large number of Haitians lack an adequate education. Only 50 percent of children in Haiti attend school, making it more difficult to find employment in the future. Haiti's school system is dominated by the non-public sector, whether for-profit, faith-based, or run by non-governmental organizations. More than 80% of primary schools are non-public, enrolling more than 80% of all primary school children. Many of them attend private or church-administered institutions. About three-fifths of the adult population can read and write. The rate of illiteracy is higher in the countryside than in the cities.

HEALTH CARE

Haiti lacks a health care system with adequate staffing, supplies, and infrastructure to meet the needs of the most remote and marginalized communities.. There is a serious shortage of health care personnel. Hospitals are severely inadequate. There are 25 physicians and 11 nurses per 100,000 population. Most rural areas have no access to health care, making residents susceptible to otherwise treatable diseases. Roughly three-fourths of Haitian households lack running water.

Unsafe water—along with unsanitary living conditions—contribute to the high incidence of infectious diseases.

WELFARE

Haiti has a history of political instability, social unrest, and natural disasters which have kept the country in poverty, thus preventing it from realizing its full potential. Poverty in Haiti is manifested by the lack of services to the population. With respect to electricity, for instance, roughly 75% of households in the country are not connected to electrical grids. The few people with access to electricity in their homes face an extremely unreliable system where the efficiency of the energy grid is approximately 50%. The population also faces the problem of lack of clean water. Today, more than half of the country's rural population still lacks access to drinkable water, while only about one-third of Haitians have access to basic sanitation

In general, however, the dearth of social programs offered by the government forced most Haitians to rely mainly on their families and on the services provided by nongovernmental organizations. As has been true in so many other areas of life, Haitians have cultivated self-reliance in the face of hardship, scarcity, and the inadequacy of existing institutions. The Haitian diaspora is presently the backbone of survival in Haiti. The diaspora has actively participated in the developmental process of the country. Haitian remittances reached $3.1 billion in 2022. Remittances are also playing a major role in helping the country.

Haiti remains this beautiful island now

inhabited by an estimated population of 11 million people. The country has long witnessed the evils of colonization, slavery, and the unfortunate sequel of oppression and dehumanization. Though Haitians had managed to overthrow the awful weight of foreign domination, they have not yet been able to build a country prosperous enough to take care of its citizenry. Haiti is a mismanaged country that still stagnates in poverty, unable to provide the basic services for the welfare of its people.

The story of my life bears witness to this rather awful situation. In the pages that follow, one will discover how I survived poverty only because I have been walking in the shadow of God's miracles.

Chapter 2

A PEACEFUL CHILDHOOD

I came into this world born in the countryside of Haiti. I give high praise to the Lord for granting grace and mercy for me to experience a healthy and peaceful childhood. I was born in Beloc Fondwa in the western part of the island. Beloc is a rural community that lacked all basic services. My mother's name was Marie Françoise Joseph. She was a homemaker. My mother exemplified a fervent devotion to the Lord throughout her life. She was well known as a missionary, in that she always left her house to go from home to home in various parts of the country to proclaim the good news of our Lord Jesus Christ.

I am the oldest of two daughters. My mother went to school in Jacmel, the main city in our department where she got an elementary education. It was there that she met my father. My mother came back home to my grandmother from Jacmel with a big surprise. She was expecting a baby. My mother told me that my grandmother was not at all happy about the fact that she had allowed that to happen to her. Since the place where they were living became too small for the impending addition to the family, my grandmother moved from Fondwa to Trouin in the area of Léogane, the next larger town in the area. There my grandmother rented a one-bedroom apartment for the extended family.

Grandmother was also very gentle and helpful to me. Since Mother was always going on the mission field, I learned to depend on Grandmother to help me as much as she could. When it came, however, to homework, Grandma was not at all able to assist me because she did not know herself how to read or write. She told me, "The only thing I can help you with is prayer." She used to make me pray so I could learn how to write Aa Bb Cc. I remember that I was left handed, but the teacher made me use my right hand. I have been punched for writing with my left hand.

I treasure wonderful memories of my childhood with my grandmother. She extended to me love and sweet affection without measure. She was a seamstress. She made clothes for people and they paid her. I remember a nice doll with fabric she once made me. She clipped my hair and applied it to the doll. There was another little girl in the neighborhood who I used to play with. When we got tired of playing with the doll, we played with a little baby dog that brought us so much fun.

My grandmother had one son who lived about two hours from our house. I think I was probably four or five years old when I went with her to visit my uncle Fernand. We got up early in the morning and started walking. We took with us some cassava which we consumed along the way for breakfast. It was always fun to go to see my uncle and have an opportunity to visit with my cousins. Their parents had a big plantation with coffee, fruits, and all kinds of vegetables. They also had a spring nearby, running down through the plantation. Grandmother and I would spend a whole week with Uncle Fernand.

I can still picture in my mind the village where I spent my young years. It was very peaceful living, with no noise of people talking loud or screaming and definitely no cars nearby. The other side of the coin is that when you live in the countryside of Haiti, you are also deprived of all basic modern commodities. For instance, one had neither watch nor a clock on the wall. You had to rely on the roosters to give you the time. In the morning, when you heard their squawking, you realized it must be six o'clock. The donkeys also took their turn in this assignment. When we heard their loud braying, we knew it must be about three in the afternoon. The cicada could be heard singing most of the night. So there were some noises, but of a different kind.

I surely enjoyed my adolescent life. I did not have toys in my childhood, but that little girl next door and I created things for our amusement. We played with grapefruits, using them as if they were animals. We put a string through their top part, and dragged them on the ground. We were content with our little dog who was so much fun to play with. Another option was going to the rivers. I felt so relaxed sitting outside under the mango tree, eagerly expecting for a mango to fall so I could eat it. It was also amusing to play with the baby birds in their nests. In those days, I didn't know what worries were. I was just living from day to day, enjoying life as it came.

It was in that little village that I started to see things that were unbelievable to me. I came to discover nature as a magnificent aspect of God's beautiful creation. To me, God's power was displayed in the many fruits I saw such as mangoes, bananas, and papayas, and all kinds of vegetables such as beans, corn, green coffee trees, and cactus trees. God's

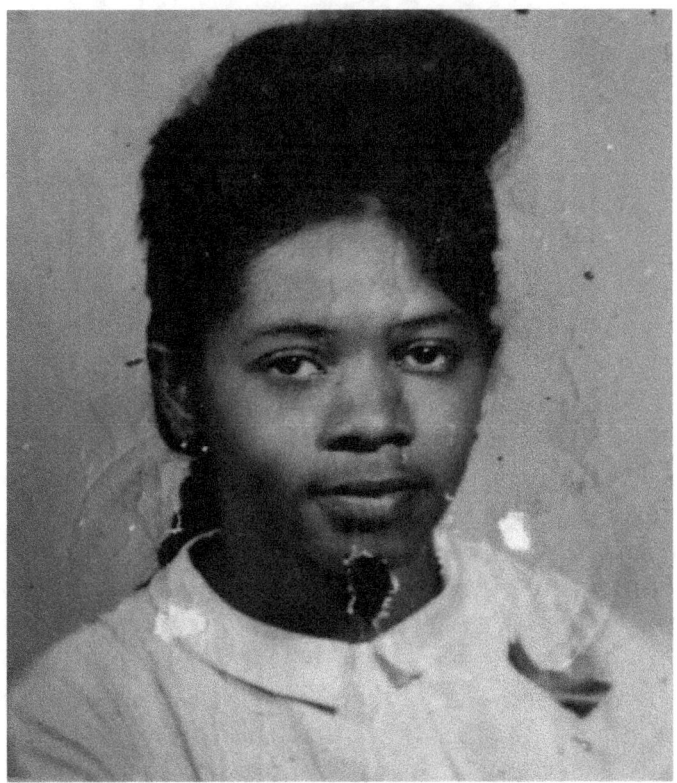

Here I am in my teen years

Another picture of my teen years

wonder in nature was displayed to me in such an amazing way.

Even playing with the chickens also gave me much joy. I came to experience, however, that playing with the baby chicks could be at time quite dangerous. I almost lost one of my eyes because the mother of the chicks hit me on my forehead when she thought I was threatening her chick. The scar still remains with me to this day, but I thank God that He protected my eyes.

Even in these early childhood years, I

experienced a divine miraculous healing in ways I could not explain. I had a sore on my ankle that couldn't be cured. There was a river not too far from the village where I resided and that's where the miracle happened. One day I put my ankle in the water and I started praying and asked God to please heal my ankle. After I finished praying and pulled my foot from the water, I gave glory to God Almighty. My ankle was completely healed.

It was about that time that God extended His gracious salvation to my mother. She was born and raised in the Catholic faith. One Sunday as she was coming home from church, the service taking place at a nearby Episcopal church caught her attention. She stopped and looked in the window of the church where she heard them singing. "Viens au Père qui t'appelle" (Come to the Father who is calling you).

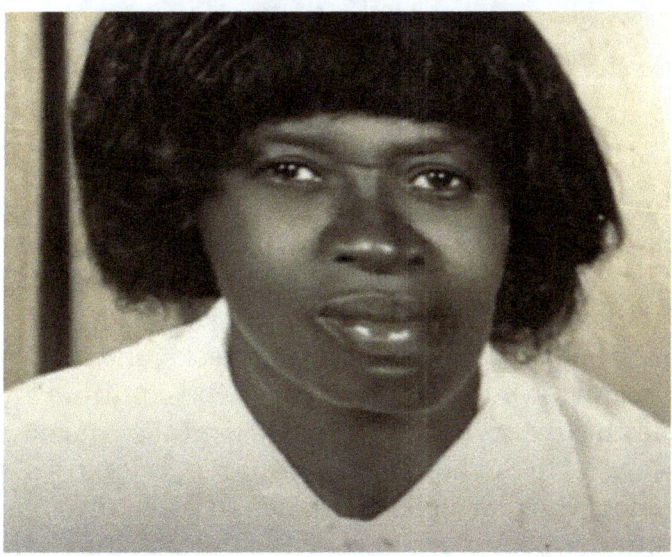

My mother, Marie Françoise Joseph, in her younger years

My grandmother, Florencia Sannon, with some of her grandchildren.

She recounted to me later how the message touched her heart. She also told me how the words of the song stayed within her.

The following week, she went back to that same Episcopal church where she gave her heart to the Lord. In later years, she moved to join a Church of God where she continued to faithfully served the Lord. My mother devoted herself to the Lord's service as a missionary. As such, she traveled from place to place throughout the provinces to pray for the sick and help those who were in need. It was during one of her trips to Port-Au-Prince that she made the decision to relocate and settle there.

As for my father, his name was Dr. Enoch Abel Gousse from Jacmel, Haiti. I would consider the stark contrasts that were present in the life of King Solomon in the Old Testament to describe my father's lifestyle. According to the Bible, Solomon was a man of "wisdom and of foolishness." One dimension of his foolishness was his sexual promiscuity. The Bible states that Solomon "had seven hundred wives, princesses, and three *hundred* concubines" (1 Kings 11:30). My father was a humble man with great talents, a man of accomplishment, but like Solomon, he was marred by moral laxity and was a womanizer.

Let me tell you more about my father, Enoch Abel Gousse. He graduated from the high school in Jacmel and then went to Calabar College in Kingston, Jamaica. He spent a year at the liberal Mount Hermon School for Boys in Massachusetts where he was the bantam-weight champion on the boxing team. In 1921, Abel enrolled at Colgate University. After graduating in 1925, he went to Syracuse University Medical School, where he completed his studies in only three years.

Despite his excellent scholastic record, he could not find work in white American hospitals. The only available place for him was the Harlem Hospital of New York that accepted him eagerly where he was promptly appointed a resident in pediatrics. Harlem at that time was undergoing a cultural revolution and Dr. Abel got to know and become friends with the leading figures of the movement. After four years at

My father, Dr. Enoch Abel Gousse, in his younger years

Harlem, he returned to Haiti in 1932, where he remained until he died. He did have a life of fulfillment for his humanitarian mission to serve his people in Haiti, eventually being considered by many Haitians to be a national treasure.

According to Dr. Gerald Oster who worked in humanitarian programs with my father, "A constant stream of patients filed into Dr. Abel Gousse's clinic on the outskirts of Jacmel. With minimal equipment and practically no funds but with considerable medical insight and lots of love, Dr. Abel, as he is lovingly called, has treated over the past 56 years nearly a million people. His medical consultations were interspersed with sessions with the elders of the Tabernacle Baptist Church of which he was the pastor. His church had 32.000 members and 103 station churches scattered over the mountains of Haiti. Through an annual visit to each one of those congregations, Dr. Abel administered spiritual as well as medical relief to the peasantry.

"Dr. Abel was a superb pediatrician. He was also the principal medical consultant of a successful self-help program designed and conducted by Selmaree Oster, called 'Osters Assurance de Santé des Enfants.' This program, which could well be a model for other Third World countries, assured health care of children in rural Haiti for a nominal fee. In their study of Haiti Children suffering from

Here I am visiting with my father

the devastating malnutrition disease "kwashiorkor."[1] Dr. Abel and the Osters discovered a simple and inexpensive treatment of supplementing the diet with copper.

When I went to visit my father in Jacmel, I spent the night there and I had the opportunity to witness his labor of love. From four in the morning, I heard a lot of people talking, and after a while they started to sing and pray. I believe that it was the time Dad started to work, and did so until three in the afternoon.

My dear mother gave me birth out of wedlock twelve years after Dad returned to Haiti. I loved and appreciated Mother for having me despite the worries and anxiety she had experienced during the time of her pregnancy. It took a spirit of grace and forgiveness to deal with that experience. Well afterwards, I am happy God made it possible for me to be alive today. My mother passed away in 2018. Thanks to my Lord and Savior Jesus Christ for paving the way for us to be reunited with her for many years. I am also very grateful to all the other moms He provided for me during my journey in life. They all served as my guardian angels. I'm grateful and blessed to be alive.

I'm also grateful to my father-in-law and mother-in-law, Pastor and Mrs. Devese Pamphile, for their love and kindness before they died. They were very faithful in doing God's work in the village where they lived, climbing mountains to help the less fortunate people in other villages. They tried their best to raise their children. I am also grateful for the

---

[1] See Abel Gousse, *A Life of Fulfillment, Haiti Observateur*, April 8-15, 1988.

sacrifices they made. Because of their good life, I was able to find a good husband who came from good roots. I thank God for grace and mercy in my favor.

Chapter 3

ORPHANAGE STAY

The realities of life in Haiti require many orphanages. An orphan is one who has lost one or both parents, but in Haiti many children were placed in orphanages because their parents were unable to care for them. The institution of an orphanage offered the chance of a better life for their children. This is the background to my early life.

The exact orphan count in Haiti has always been unreliable. The House of Hope in Gonaïves in the Artibonite area has claimed that Haiti has an estimated 1.2 million orphans and vulnerable children, with about 7,000 children roaming the streets of Port-au-Prince. Thousands more can be found across the island in cities such as Cap Haitien, St. Marc, and Gonaives. Whatever the exact number, the orphanage system was created (and continues to exist) due to a combination of poverty, natural disasters, physical/intellectual disabilities, inadequate housing, and a lack of health and education services. Combine all that with the occurrence of sexual promiscuity—fathers refusing to take responsibility and single mothers unable to cope—and you can see why children have always been exposed to a high risk of harm, abuse, and trafficking.

Mother took me to an orphanage when I was about seven years old. When she gave birth to a second daughter, it was difficult for her to make ends meet without a job or any income. What's more, my father had abandoned us. I had been fortunate enough to attend a Catholic school that was free for us. Even better, they had a canteen, so I was able to get meals, but the burden on my mother was great.

Miss Doris Burke, an older lady from Jamaica, had founded this orphanage, and while not well maintained, it was not considered poorly run. I remember that for the first month I had to sleep on the floor without sheets or pillow—there was no bed for me. My first bed I shared with another little girl.

There is a memory that remains with me after all these years. There were two unrelated children, probably one-year-olds, sharing a crib. Their names were Irma and Shaugy. These two children were always in the crib, day and night, and no one seemed to care for them. They only came out of the crib when there was an inspection. I can still see them standing together holding each other's hand.

Then there was a time around ten one night when I went out to the clothesline when a big black pig came running at me. As I remember, it resembled a bear. I screamed so loudly that I woke the other children who began screaming as well. It was quite a time before we all calmed down. Even with such drama, strong relationships were formed amongst us, with some relationships lasting over the years. There are three girls with whom I have remained in close contact and we occasionally call one another to reminisce.

After a year and a half at the orphanage, Mrs. Burke decided to take some of us on a vacation to Cahook Anse-A Vaux in southern Haiti. What fun we had living right by the ocean. Although I could not swim, and there was no lifeguard, we spent most of the time playing in the ocean. I do remember getting very sick with bronchitis, and receiving herb tea, after which I was healed within a week.

I had really hoped that on my return to Port-au-Prince, I would not have to go back to that same orphanage. My prayers were answered as Mother Exumé took three of us to a newly-created orphanage, the brainchild of both Bishop Charles H. Mason and Mother Dorothy Webster Exumé. I was just a nine-year old child, but I recognized the profound influence on our lives from both Bishop Mason and Mother Exumé. They opened up the word of God to me through the actions of their everyday lives.

I was home-schooled for a year until Mother Exumé moved to Pétion-Ville due to the political instability in Port-au-Prince. Here I was able to attend public school for my elementary education, before attending a lycée for my high school years. The political tension in Haiti hung over us like a black cloud during those years. At times, we were under a curfew. I well remember a man looking for mangoes in the early morning so he could feed his family. He was shot by the police in front of the orphanage, the stain of his blood remaining there for days.

How my biological father came back into my life in my adolescent years is a story worth telling. I had visited the public clinic in the town of Pétion-Ville for a regular checkup. After reporting for triage, I gave the clerk Rose-Marie my name. She asked for my last name, as well as my father's name, and then she paused. What occurred next was truly miraculous. I went back to the orphanage to tell the other children that I had met a half-sister. They were all spellbound with excitement.

Three months after this surprising encounter, my sister came to pick me up from the orphanage, but the supervisor refused to release me. Later, my father himself came to the orphanage—that was the first day I met him. This well-dressed man gave me a big hug and spent half of the morning talking to me and the orphanage supervisor. I was very happy to get to know this man, my father. I had packed my bags, but I was not allowed to go with him.

From that day on, he included me in the long list of his children, giving me a birth certificate. Previously I had carried my mother's last name but when my father officially recognized me, I no longer used the name Joseph, but called myself Marie Rozelle Gousse.

My unmarried father was both a medical doctor and a pastor at a Baptist church in Jacmel. He asked me to forgive him for failing to take care of me in my early life. Deep in my heart, I believe Dad was a good man. I was too young to be a judge of anyone's sinful life but looking back, he did seem sorry for his lack of moral maturity. Upon further reflection, I have concluded that the best gift given to me was the miracle of life from both my mother and father.

The orphanage had changed location again, this time to a different house in the same town, located near to a dry river bank. The house was a Spanish-style building with four porches, two upstairs and two downstairs with iron grills on all four of them. To go to the second floor, we had to go outside. Some of the children slept upstairs and the older ones, including me, slept downstairs. It was there that I had an experience that opened up my awareness of God's presence.

One night in a dream, I saw a brown cow trying to get through the second-story window which was by the steps, so we had no escape. I suddenly awoke from my dream, jumped up and ran to the front door, opened it, and walked down. I was no longer afraid, I heard a voice telling me not to look behind. Again, the voice talked to me, telling me to sing, "I need Thee every hour." I knew at that moment I needed to live in God's presence, for I could do nothing without Him. When I knocked on the door, one of the girls opened it without even asking who was at the door. Upon entering, I was thinking of yet another song to sing, but one of girls had begun to sing "I need Thee every hour."

It was around 2:00 that morning, but everyone was up, singing, praying and praising the Lord. I shared my dream with them all. Suddenly as I looked on the one porch that overlooked the ravine, I saw three men with

Marie-Rozelle Gousse at 13 years old

three cows, cows like the one I had seen in my dream. All three men had red scarves around their necks and each carried what looked like a cowboy's whipping cord in their hands. Everyone at the orphanage got up early each day for prayer, the weapon of our survival. We had to keep hope alive through prayers and fasting, always thanking God for His love.

There was yet another miracle I experienced at the orphanage. We only had powdered milk and cheese to eat. The assistant supervisor told us we were going to fast that day and pray for food to come to our table. The older children removed all the furniture in the

Here are the orphanage children. I am standing on the top right side next to the little girl on the ledge.

living room, put sheets on the floor, and started to pray. Within two hours a member from the Church World Service arrived at the orphanage for a visit. He had been unable to work because thoughts of the orphanage filled his mind. So, he went out and bought one hundred pounds of beans and one hundred pounds of rice to bring to the orphanage as a gift.

A short while later, two men arrived with big baskets of bread and cookies. One was the man in charge of the Tontons Macoutes (President Duvalier's secret police) who owned a bakery. He had been thinking of the orphanage though he did not know why.

The last visitor was a lady who worked as an interpreter for tourists. She was passing by the orphanage and stopped when she heard

Here I am in my early 20s in Haiti

us praying and then gave us money for charcoal. All we needed was to have faith in God. It seemed to me that the Lord Jesus had watched over me every second of my life, always directing my footsteps.

The Lord Jesus has watched over me every second of my life. He directed my footsteps. His word is right and remains very relevant for us: "Trust in the Lord with all your heart and lean not on your own understanding; in all your ways, acknowledge him, he will direct your path" (Proverbs 3:5-6). God is real and if you trust in Him with all your heart and might, your life will be blessed in every way.

That is what I learned as a young child and I have not strayed from that realization even now that I am a grandmother. God's provision for me continued as you will read in the next chapter as I tell of how God opened the door for me to come to the U.S.

Chapter 4

COMING TO AMERICA

My adoptive mother, Dorothy Webster Exume, was a very dynamic woman of God. She was born in Cleveland, Ohio and was a graduate from Case Western Reserve University in Ohio with a B.A degree in sociology and a double minor in French and English. Her specialized training enabled her to teach French in the Cleveland public school system.

Mother Exumé was consumed by the desire to engage in mission works from an early age. That desire became a reality when International Supervisor Mother Lilian Brooks Coffey and Bishop Charles H. Mason, founder of the Church of God in Christ, gave their approval for her to serve in Haiti. On July 2, 1947, Mother Exumé arrived in Port-au-Prince as a missionary. She would remain in the country for three decades and was instrumental in changing and influencing many lives.

The establishing of the orphanage was one of her greatest achievements in Haiti.

Leon, Dad Helman, Rose Ellen and I at the Pittsburgh Theological Seminary

One of the primary sites of this institution was Pétion-Ville, a suburb of metropolitan Port-au-Prince. I was one of the daughters at the orphanage who was transformed through her love and care. Mother Exume taught us how to pray and also imparted to us the etiquette required for a successful lifestyle.

I spent several years at the orphanage and miracles followed me thereto. I had a dream when I was sixteen years old in which I saw a small boat coming toward me from the distance over a calm ocean. When it got closer to me from where I was standing, the little boat became a short man standing on the ocean who asked me to come with him. He told me he was taking me to a different country. So I did walk on the ocean platform until I saw a bright light.

Then he said, "This is where we are planning to go." I opened my eyes and when I came to myself, I realized that it was just a dream.

Mother Exumé had a great network of supporters and friends who often visited the orphanage. Foreign missionaries regularly came to spend time with the children, providing compassionate words of encouragement. One day, a group of them were so touched by what they saw that they promised to work to obtain scholarships for the three oldest among us to study in the United States.

Upon leaving Haiti, these missionaries kept their word. They set out to work on

Coming to America

the necessary papers to obtain the visas so we could come to America. Within a year, all three of us had appointments to go to the American embassy to meet with the consul for visas. Unfortunately, we were turned down because the paperwork application for the scholarship was filled out for us to go to Mississippi. In the '60s, Mississippi, a state in the deep South, was a hotbed for racism. Being well aware of this situation, the consul decided not to send us to that place.

God by no means gave up on us. He opened a new door for us, for He is the God of miracles and opportunities. When He closes a door, He opens another one. Alexander Graham Bell said, "We often look so long and so regretfully upon the closed door that we do not see the one which has opened for us." God opened another door through a gracious missionary couple who had committed themselves to help Haiti and its people. They were members of the Brethren Church in Bradenton, Florida by the name of Leslie and Fern Helman. The Lord sent our way this remarkable couple.

Mr. Helman gave special support to a feeding station in Port-au-Prince called "Aide Aux Enfants" (Aid To Children) coordinated by then Pastor Luc Nérée, a Baptist preacher and leader. When they came to the orphanage, they took a special interest in me. One day, they returned to the orphanage and asked Mother Exumé if they could help one of three older girls with a scholarship to study in the United States. Obviously, Mother Exumé was very happy for that offer. They would subsequently help me leave Haiti to join them in the United States.

After three months or so, the Helmans came back to Haiti. They brought with them three dresses, one for each of the three girls—two were blue and one had different colors of bright orange, green, and red flowers. Mrs. Helman gave me the bright dress and the blue ones to the other girls. The Helman said they will take the girl with the bright dress to the State and I would stay with them while I went to school there.

My dream came true, and that was my miracle. This time, the consul gave me the visa to come. I landed in the United States on March 15, 1968, an unforgettable day in my life. The dream I had long held in my mind and thoughts became a reality. It was a day of excitement. Mother Dorothy Exumé had done an incredible job to secure food and raiment for the girls. Yet these things were not always readily available for us. I was infinitely glad to move away from the life of the orphanage where it was difficult to satisfy even the most basic necessities of life.

It was also a date of painful separation from the girls I had been connected with all my youthful days. They were all my sisters. We grew together through many years of common joys and acute adversity. We experienced together all the vicissitudes of life. We prayed together and cried to God to intervene to soften the burdens of a hard and sometimes miserable life.

Still we counted our blessings. We were able to go to school while many other girls we knew were not actually granted this

Orphanage founder Dr. Dorothy Exume

opportunity. It was indeed a painful moment to part from them. The Lord did intervene for the other two girls when another benefactor helped them travel to Canada where both studied nursing and enjoyed a rewarding career.

It was especially difficult to leave behind my mother Françoise and my only biological sister, Elvire. Though we did not live together under one roof, we still maintained a pretty close relationship. They came to visit me, and I was also allowed occasionally to leave the orphanage walls to visit with my mother. It was particularly hard to leave behind my boyfriend, Leon. He has been a great support for me in many ways. We enjoyed each other's company when possible.

The flight out of Port-au-Prince was scheduled for the early evening. I was very anxious to go to the airport. Mother Exumé drove me there and stayed with me until boarding time. She made arrangements with a friend of hers, Mrs. Lula Bowman, to pick me up in Miami. Upon arriving, Mrs Bowman who was waiting, quickly identified me, exclaiming "This is my little girl." I stayed at her house for a week until I left for my destination to the Helman's house. In Miami, it was amazing to discover what I could consider as a new world. Indeed I was dumbfounded as I discovered skyscrapers, neat neighborhoods, and clean streets. Everything looked so different from what I had left back in Haiti.

After a few weeks in Miami, the time came for me to move to my final destination. The Helmans came to pick me up from Bradenton on the other side of the state. What a privilege it was to embark on this new stage of my life with them! They were very kind and treated me like their own child. I will never forget their love and kindness to me. The Helmans worshiped at the Brethren Church in Bradenton.

Dr. Martin Luther King Jr. once said that 11 a.m. on Sunday morning was the most segregated hour in America. This was true for the Brethren Church in Bradenton. It was an altogether white congregation. The Helmans had to ask permission from the pastor before I could worship there. There was a church member that said if a black person ever entered their sanctuary, he would leave the church. But

Mr. and Mrs. Helman

before the very Sunday I was to attend service there, he died. We continued to worship there every Sunday. The pastor and other members were nice to me. It was a wonderful journey with Mother and Dad Helman. I thank God for their love and their families.

    I did experience other racial incidents, but God was always good and gave me strength to endure every situation. Through His unfailing love and faithful help, I survived them all. I was at the Helmans the night Dr. Martin Luther King Jr. was gunned down. I remember that I was watching a program on TV when a news flash came on announcing his murder.

    Because of a racist remark someone had

made to me earlier that day, I was already very burdened. It felt like a heavy black cloud was hanging over my left shoulder. Then I asked Mother Helman who the principal black leader in America was. She explained to me the life and works of Dr. King. She asked me if I knew about him. My answer was I had never heard of him before.

Then she asked me what was the reason for asking her that question, I told her that I felt that leader needed prayer right now. She said she could not get in touch with him because she would not have his information. Suddenly later that very night came this breaking news on TV reporting that Dr. King has been shot. Mother Helman could not believe I had seen something like this so clearly that trouble was coming. These big black clouds I had experienced were signs of unrest. The Helmans had me watch all the reports and events connected with this terrible tragedy caused by hateful people. But with God's help, my pains were relieved.

The Helmans had a couple that came to visit with them one time. Mother Helman told me that they were from the KKK. For some reason, she did not want me to go in my room. She wanted me to sit in the living room with them during their visit. After thirty minutes, since I could not understand the conversation, I got up and went to my room. She still came to get me to come back to the living room. She wanted me to be included in their company despite their racial attitude. Dad and Mother Helman were very gracious to me.

One other incident that happened was quite significant in shoring up my confidence

My early days in Miami

in God. The Helman had two homes, one in Florida, and the other at the Indian Lake, Ohio. From a previous marriage, Mother Helman had grown-up children and one of them came once to visit her mother. It happened that he came on a weekend Saturday night. After some conversation, he promised to take me to church the following Sunday. I said I would be happy to go to church with him. But before going to to bed, I watched him cleaning up his guns.

    As planned, we did go to church in the morning. On my way back, he drove me into a forest. When he reached to a certain area, he asked me to get out of the car. I told him I did not have any reason to get out of the car. When he insisted, I told him I would never leave the car until we get back home. As I sat there in the car, I made sure my seatbelt was tightly fastened. I really didn't know what his intention was, but I'm glad I stood my ground.

God's hand of protection surrounded me. I stood on His wonderful promise in the twenty third psalm: "Though I walk through the valley of the shadow of death, I fear no evil, for you are with me. Your rod and your staff, they comfort me" (Psalm 23:3-4). I have also stood on the seven powerful promises the Lord made to us in Psalm 91 throughout my life:

> *"Because he loves me, says the Lord, I will rescue him I will protect him, for he acknowledges my name He will call upon me and I will answer him I will be with him in trouble I protect him and deliverer him and honor him With long life, I will satisfy him and will show him my salvation"* (Psalm 91:15-16).

Thanks be to God for His angels who has always encamped all around me.

I came to know a woman who was a member of the KKK from Mississippi. When she came to visit the house, she would never speak to me, not even say good morning. I did not let people with that kind of attitude get under my skin. I knew so well that selfishness, hatred, jealousy, and ignorance are evil. I also knew that God had a plan for my life. My assurance was firmly grounded in God's provisions as described in Psalm's 103. Like David, I counted all the blessings the Lord has bestowed on me:

Early days in Miami

> *He forgave all my iniquities*
> *He healed my disease*
> *He rescued my life from the pit*
> *And crowned me with loving-kindness and tender mercies.*
> *He satisfies my desires with good things so that my youth is renewed like the eagle* (Psalm 103:4-5).

Most members of the Helman's family were very nice and kind to me: the grandchildren and the neighbors. I'm still in touch with one of their granddaughters. They treated me just as if I was their own daughter. I'm very grateful to the Helman family. I had a lot of fun with them.

In Ohio, we were living right in front

of the Indian Lake. Dad and Mother had a boat. They let me pilot it when they were in it. Sometimes in the afternoon, I sat right in front of the lake fishing and caught some nice catfish. My stay in Huntsville, Ohio was for me amazing and unforgettable.

I credit this wonderful experience to the grace of our Lord. I had learned to stand on God's promises since I can bear abundant witness of their fulfillment in my life. Yes, when I'm standing on God's promises, I know I cannot fall. I thank God for His miracles that allowed me to see His goodness, and experience in such a personal way His daily protection.

… Chapter 5

TYING THE KNOT WITH THE LOVE OF MY LIFE

I met my good friend, Leon Dénius Pamphile, when I was living at the Church of God in Christ orphanage in Pétion-Ville. I was then a teenager of fourteen years old while he was nineteen. He was in his last year of secondary education. The orphanage took the children for a day of recreation on a boat to which the Church Of God In Christ youth were also invited. So it was the day when we had a chance to talk.

He asked me if I would like to be his best friend in life but I told him no. He did not give up after my initial response but wrote me a nice letter, asking me again to be his friend. I wrote back after a week and said that I would.

He was not allowed to visit but we became friends. He used to write some beautiful

Our early romance

letters to me. Our romance was never a secret to the other children at the orphanage even though contact between us remained limited. Since there wasn't any telephone available at that time, exchanging letters became our primary source of communication, and those letters nurtured and strengthened our love for one another. He found another opportunity for us to meet, for the mail for the orphanage came to his house in Port-au-Price. Therefore, he was always the one to bring it to the orphanage. That was a golden opportunity for us to see each other.

I had other eyes on me so I had to ask the Lord to show me a sign that Leon was the right person for me. I asked that if he was the one that my heart would beat faster the next time I saw him. Then I would know he was the right person for me. Well, that's what really happened. One day I saw him and my heart was racing so fast that I had to stop to thank God for answering my prayer. Ask the Lord in faith for whatever you need, and He will grant you your requests.

I thank God for helping me to make the best choice of a husband for my life. I had seen in him the character of a good man. As it is written in God's word, "Love the Lord your God with all your heart and with all your soul and with all your strength" (Deuteronomy 6:5). I realized that Leon loved the Lord. Also, there were other good character traits in him, such as honesty, politeness, and kindness that radiated from his personality. He is a man that usually stands in the gap through prayer for others, a man of noble character.

He loves to read and study the word of God. He is also a hard worker, very honest, always smiling, and a man with a clean mind. He is always trying to help someone. He is well trained with a degree in law from the University of Haiti, a master's degree from the Pittsburgh Theological Seminary and a Ph.D. in education from the University of Pittsburgh. He has written several books and articles on education in Haiti and the relations between Haiti and the United States. The Lord led me to make the right choice. Thanks be to God for my husband's spirit of obedience.

After two years or so, he was allowed to visit me at the orphanage with a chaperone. About that time, his mother and dad came to the orphanage to talk to the supervisor, Mother Dorothy W. Exume, to ask for my hand in marriage. It was some serious talk about their son to be in love with one of her

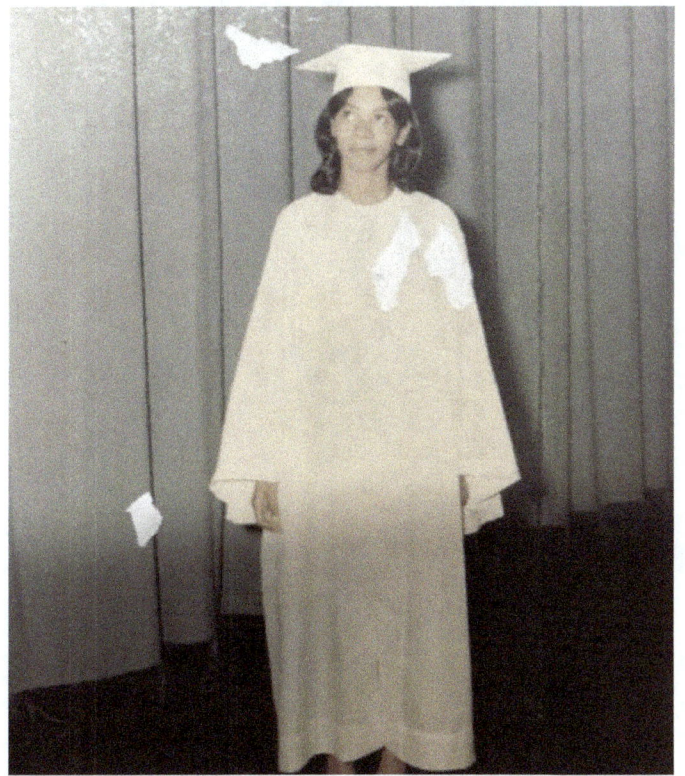
Receiving my high school diploma

orphanage daughters and after that, it became public knowledge that I was in love with Leon Pamphile. When the time came to emigrate to the United States to be with the Helmans, we had that ultimate meeting two days before I left in a nearby galette (dry river bed) where I promised him I would be faithful and keep my heart just for him.

    Upon traveling to Bradenton, I wanted to complete my high school diploma. Mother Helman got someone to translate all my papers from French into English. I went to Manatee Junior College in Sarasota Florida for a year

Our wedding picture - August 1969

where I earned my GED. Having completed this process, I was doing my very best to get on with my life. I applied to a cosmetology school in Palmetto, Florida. I was accepted, but a brand new perspective burst onto my horizon. The new direction was exciting because my best friend asked me to marry him. By then, Leon had finished his studies in Haiti, having graduated from Law School and the Ecole Normale Supérieure (School of Education). He was then ready to enter into matrimony with me. I said yes to him. I came back to Haiti and we got married.

I shared my new plan with Dad and

Mother Helman. They were also happy for me. They told the pastor and his wife who would announce it to the church. They showed great appreciation for us by having two showers for me. Mother and Dad Helman purchased my wedding dress and all the accessories. God's miracles were shadowing and following me every step of the way. Leon and I were happy as God enabled us to keep our promises to each other.

After our wedding, I returned to Miami, not to the Helmans. I was able to work there while making plans for Leon to join me. It took more than a year to get his papers in order and he was finally able to come to the

Our 25th wedding anniversary

U.S. in December 1970. Miracles followed us again when God used a beautiful family who graciously extended their support to us. Their names were Mr. and Mrs. Alfred Joseph and they welcomed us into their home. The next step on our trajectory brought us to Pittsburgh, Pennsylvania.

Dr. Bennie and Mary Ellen Godwin had come to Haiti in the previous years as missionaries. During their stay, they became acquainted with Leon who served as interpreter and guide for them. A solid friendship developed through this encounter. Bennie Godwin was a recruiter for the Pittsburgh Theological Seminary. After Leon arrived in Florida, Bennie recruited him as a student for the Pittsburgh Theological Seminary. Leon came to Pittsburgh before me to enroll for classes on the very last day of December 1970. By then, I was expecting our first child.

When I flew to Pittsburgh in 1971, it was the beginning of a brand new adventure. It was the first time in my life I experienced winter. It was awfully cold and it was my first time seeing snow. It looked truly beautiful. God's miraculous grace continued to overshadow us. People of goodwill brought us their benevolent support. There were some members from the South Hills Presbyterian church who were quite supportive of us. They had a baby shower for us and invited us to come to various activities, including dinner with other families. One of the ladies named Cindy was just like a sister to us. Now you see what I mean when I say that miracles followed me wherever I went.

God constantly provided friends for us

and the following spring I gave birth to a beautiful baby girl. I am so grateful to God for He cares for us. The couple that were our sponsors to Pittsburgh Seminary were also kind and helpful to us. Mrs. Goodwin was like a big sister to my new family. She arranged everything for us and became my daughter's godmother.

I found employment at the Seminary in the mail room as a printer and address-ographer. My husband was in school both at the Seminary and the University of Pittsburgh. He worked part-time at a private school in the Allison Park suburb of Pittsburgh. He has worked hard all throughout his life. He graduated with high honors from the Seminary.

Leon told me then that when the Lord blessed us, we would start helping Haiti. He asked me how I felt about the suggestion and I said I thought it was a very good idea. This plan became a reality as we established an organization named the Functional Literacy Ministry with the mission to provide education, health care, and hope to Haitians. To God be the glory. I will share about our ministry later in this book.

Chapter 6

WALKING WITH JESUS

Salvation occupies a fundamental place in the successful life of an individual. It's grounded in God's precious gift of His Son to build a new relationship with Him: "For God so loved the world that he gave his only Son that whoever believes in him should not perish but have everlasting life (John 3:16). Salvation through Christ is the only means of empowerment to live a purposeful life here on earth and also make it to heaven on the last day.

Salvation produces a brand new birth. It leads to the beginning of a new life, empowering you with new thoughts resulting in new behavior: "If anyone is in Christ, he is a new creation. The old has gone. The new has come" (2 Corinthians 5:17).

I am so blessed to have access to this new life in Christ. I got saved at a young age. My salvation stands prominently as one of the greatest miracles in my life. I was sitting in the courtyard of our small and humble home, enjoying the shade of a mango tree facing our neighbor's kitchen. In the countryside of Haiti, you usually have an outdoor kitchen. Our neighbor was an older lady in her late fifties. I remember well seeing her smoking in a hidden place. I was playing around that area before I sat down at the foot of the tree.

While sitting there, I suddenly heard a loud voice say to me, "If you just say Jesus, he will answer." I turned around looking all over but I could not see anyone. So I did not answer. The voice again repeated the same message: "If you just say Jesus, he will answer." I still did not respond. I became afraid as I looked all around me and could not see anyone close by. Suddenly the lady that was smoking in the kitchen came out and said "Jesus." I heard the voice answering very loudly, "Yes, my child." From then on, I gained the full confidence that Jesus is real. Jesus is the compassionate God who forgave me and has not given up on me.

Later in my life, I discovered the message of the prophet Joel: "Anyone who calls on the name of the Lord will be saved" (Joel 2:32). No matter how sinful and disobedient we have been, we can receive God's forgiveness by turning to Him in repentance. God's love is powerful and eternal. Praise be His holy name. God still shows me that He has been with me in so many ways. From that moment on, I became a believer and no one can ever take this name off my heart. I have forever believed that God is real and He is loving and powerful.

I always regret that I missed that opportunity to answer the precious voice of Jesus. Yet I know full well that "because of the Lord's great love we are not consumed, for *his*

My mother, Marie Françoise Joseph, and I

compassions never fail" (Lamentations 3:22). By His mercies we have been kept from complete destruction. Jesus still shows mercy on me (see Romans 9:15-16). God said to Moses, "I will show mercy on whom I will show mercy" (Exodus 33:19). So receiving God's promise is not up to us. We can't get it by working hard for it. In any way, God will show mercy to anyone He chooses. He had mercy on me. He continues to bless me and use me.

    I feel so blessed because of the Christian upbringing I received from my family. My grandmother and mother were very faithful in their walk with Jesus. They cared about my education and took me regularly to Sunday School. I accompanied them when they attended morning prayer meetings. From the early stage of my life, I was very well grounded in building my faith in Jesus Christ as my Lord and Savior. I always believed in the power of the Holy Spirit.

We lived in a very small village with very few houses, with an outside kitchen, and a big yard surrounded by all kinds of trees. It was in this atmosphere of quietness and peace that one night I had a dream. I saw a ladder that came down from the sky close to me. There was a man holding the ladder with a hose in his hands. He then handed it to me and he asked me to sprinkle the earth. I told my mother the dream the next day. She told me the Lord had chosen me for a special mission. I didn't think of it until I got older. I came to realize that I was chosen to serve God and sprinkle His blessings like water on the lives of others. The Lord had put His seal on me at an early age.

The church we attended was located in our small village, thirty minutes walking distance from our house. The loving pastor was truly saved. He was filled with the Holy Spirit, a joyful and prayerful man. There is a wonderful testimony I recall happening in that church. Our area was in the midst of a dry season with no rain for many weeks. One Sunday morning, the pastor said he would not preach that day, but would instead pray until God sent us the rain. He led the congregation in a strong and fervent prayer of faith. The Lord answered as rain poured out from heaven. It was a joyful and exciting Sunday to witness how God showed His faithfulness toward His promises. As a child, it was for me a miracle that greatly reinforced my belief in my Lord and Savior Jesus Christ.

As I grew older and attended different schools, my views and my faith about my Savior have remained unshakable. Back then at the orphanage, we had to walk one hour to church. It was very hard because the sun was hot, but we made it by the grace of God. Later on, we found a church that was not as far: the Assembly of God Church in Pétion-Ville. The other girls and I were old enough to join the choir at that church. I went to the baptism class and God convinced me it was the right thing to do to get baptized, so I did. It is amazing when you have faith in Jesus Christ. God's promises become real to you day by day: "Believe on the Lord Jesus and you will be saved along with your entire household" (Acts 16:31). I thank God for saving me.

As a child of God, I feel so well protected by the mighty power of my Lord and Savior Jesus Christ. After we moved to Pittsburgh, my husband and I joined the Lincoln Avenue Church of God. We fell in love with that congregation because of its warm fellowship and inspiring style of worship. It was a loving environment and a good place for our children. I got involved in different activities. What I enjoyed the most at that church was the joyful and enthusiastic singing. They worshiped as in the Haitian churches we had left behind. I was always eager to attend the Wednesday night prayer meetings.

Working as a press operator at Matthias Copy Quick

There a was a miracle that took place in Pittsburgh that reaffirmed my faith even more strongly. I was looking for employment. I applied at a place and was called for an interview. The night before I went, my mother, who had come to be with me, had a dream of the person who would interview me for the job. My mother gave me a good description of that person as seen in her dream. When I went for the interview, I found a lady who I felt I already knew because of what my mother had told me. I found favor with her and she hired me as a printer right on the spot.

Although I was working, my husband needed a better job to support our family. He had just finished his studies at the Seminary and was working part time as a translator for the Dravo Corporation in downtown Pittsburgh. At that time, God granted him favor and here's how. I was invited to lead the

Wednesday night prayer meeting at a church. I prayed for those who were in need of employment. The next day, there was a phone call to my house from the Pittsburgh Board of Education. My mother who was home alone answered the call and took the phone number exactly as it was given to her. We considered this a miracle because she spoke very little English. When my husband called the Board, they asked him to come for an interview. He was hired to teach French and Spanish.

I learned to lean strongly on my Savior Jesus Christ for everything I needed. I have always served God with a humble spirit. While we were at Lincoln Avenue Church of God, my husband launched a ministry to help Haitians called the Functional Literacy Ministry of Haiti (FLM Haiti). The goal is to provide education, health care and hope to the needy and disadvantaged. The Lord has immensely blessed this ministry to empower us to help make life better for countless people in Haiti.

My husband later accepted a pastoral position to lead the First Church of God of New Kensington in the outskirts of Pittsburgh. I joined him in the work and again became very active in the church. I had the privilege of serving as Sunday School superintendent. Besides being a pastor, my husband continued to serve as the executive director of the Functional Literacy Ministry of Haiti. He has traveled back and forth to Haiti on mission trips and helped his dad with his Church. After a few years of serving the church in New Kensington, he was chosen and had agreed to serve as the bishop of the Church of God In

Christ (COGIC) in Haiti. Since then the Lord continues to use us as channels of the blessings for the ministry of the COGIC-Haiti.

It is a blessing to serve and help those who need an extended hand. The good Lord has blessed me tremendously in every way and I felt I should share my blessings with others. I'm very grateful to my Lord and Savior Jesus Christ.

I am also grateful to everyone who reached out to touch my life. I am happy that the Lord extended His hand and pulled me through many dangers and snares. I give thanks to God for saving me. I give thanks for my husband for being so kind and patient with me. I give thanks God for my biological family and the family of God.

Chapter 7

EXPERIENCING GOD'S HEALING MIRACLES

Divine healing involves a supernatural act which resolves a physical, emotional, or spiritual problem. Examples of the miraculous healing power of God are evident throughout the Bible. Approximately one-fifth of the gospel narrative is devoted to Jesus' healing ministry. At the start of His ministry, Jesus "went throughout Galilee, teaching in their synagogues, preaching the good news of the kingdom, and healing every disease and sickness among the people" (Matthew 4:23).

I have a special interest in the dramatic story in the Old Testament of how God showed evidence of His compassion for Hezekiah by healing him. It is recorded that in those days when Hezekiah fell ill and was at the point of death, a prophet paid him a visit:

> In those days Hezekiah was sick and near death. And Isaiah the prophet,

the son of Amoz, went to him and said to him, "Thus says the Lord: 'Set your house in order, for you shall die, and not live.'"

Then he turned his face toward the wall, and prayed to the Lord, saying, "Remember now, O Lord, I pray, how I have walked before You in truth and with a loyal heart, and have done *what was* good in Your sight." And Hezekiah wept bitterly.

And it happened, before Isaiah had gone out into the middle court, that the word of the Lord came to him, saying, "Return and tell Hezekiah the leader of My people, 'Thus says the Lord, the God of David your father: "I have heard your prayer, I have seen your tears; surely I will heal you. On the third day you shall go up to the house of the Lord" (2 Kings 20:1-5).

Hezekiah did not accept the report about his health and life and instead turned to the Lord. God promised to heal him and God never goes back on His promises.

God healed Hezekiah as He promised he would. I use this passage of Scripture to demonstrate that God's miracles have been working for others over the centuries, long before I was born. God is still the same, intervening on our behalf when we find ourselves overwhelmed by trouble of all kinds. He has also done for me miracles for which I remain thankful.

The very first time I became aware of

My mother, Marie Joseph, and I

God's miraculous power was when I was only five years old and living with my grandmother and mother. As I mentioned earlier, I had a terrible sore on my left ankle that could not be healed. One day I went to the river where I often played. I let my ankle soak in a special part of the river and I started to pray. I asked the Lord to please heal my ankle, and not to let me return home with that sore. After my foot soaked for a little while, I took it out of the water. I was happy to realize that my ankle was completely healed and my skin was restored to its natural condition. I was completely cleansed from that infection.

It is amazing what God can do if we trust Him with all our heart and mind. He is there to help and protect us. I sang for joy all the way back home because God had done something special for me. My mother and grandmother also marveled at how the Lord had healed my wounds that had lasted for so long. Praise God from whom all blessings flow. God kept His promise to me of healing.

Then later God visited me with a second memorable miraculous healing. I can remember a time when I felt so sick. I had quite a case of whooping cough and the coughing was awful. I also vomited after I ate. In the community where I lived, there were no clinics or any kind of medical facilities. People in the village had to depend on God and natural remedies. My grandmother felt sorry for me. One day after the church service, one of the missionaries told Mother what to do for me so I could get well. She advised her not to let me know about what she was going to be doing because she feared I might not want it.

She gave my mother a recipe consisting of killing a mouse and cooking it for me to eat. She was to wash it with lime and salt, dry it in the sun for a day, grill it very well, and let me eat it. Mother did all that without me knowing about her preparation. After grilling it, she told me she had prepared something for me. When I got to the kitchen, I saw this grilled meat which I was very happy to eat without knowing what it was.

After I finished consuming it, Mom told me what it was. I was surprised because it was so delicious. But it was only days later that I became aware of the reason for my mother's action. I was restored back to health, running around the yard and playing as usual. I am so glad that God used even simple things like that to help me. I was under the mighty power of a great Doctor, my Lord and Savior Jesus Christ. He was and has always been there for me.

About five years ago, I experienced the most horrible sickness in my life. My husband was in Haiti on a mission for the Church of God in Christ. I felt very weak and couldn't

Mother Exume with children at her former orphanage in Canada

walk very fast. I sometimes felt like I was going to pass out and I was losing a lot of weight. At the time, Mother was in a nursing home. When I went to see her, she told me I didn't look good. I told her I was okay but she shook her head and was unconvinced. When I returned home, I sat on the couch for a long time until I could drag myself upstairs. That feeling of weakness beset me all week long.

I finally had one of my adopted daughters with me on Sunday by the name of Niandra Loiseau. We decided to attend the service at the Morningside Church of God In Christ. While at church, I felt very sick to my stomach. Realizing my discomfort, Niandra asked me what was wrong. I told her I probably ate something that had upset my stomach. After church, she came home with me. We had dinner together before I took her home. On Monday, I was still miserable and in pain.

My strength continued to decline and by Wednesday my energy was so low that I had trouble putting my clothes on. Every time I sat down, I fell asleep on the couch. My sister, who came to visit with me that Wednesday afternoon, said she was going to call my children to let them know of my condition. I told her not to because I would be okay. She left and did call my one of my daughters. I had another adopted spiritual daughter who called me and I told her I was not feeling well. She called my husband in Haiti who urged me to see my regular doctor. When I went to the doctor as a walk-in, the receptionist asked me to come next week.

Through it all, I was covered and protected by divine power: "The angel of the Lord encamps around those that fear him and delivers them" (Psalm 34:7). On Thursday night, I decided to go to the hospital. When I tried to dress up, I could not do it. Every time I started, I fell back on the bed and fell asleep. At 2 a.m., I mustered the little strength I still had to put my clothes on. The Lord helped me to drive to the hospital. When I finally made it to the emergency room, they attended to me right away.

Upon examining my condition, the doctor found out that I was losing blood internally. My blood count was very low and they gave me three pints of blood. My diagnosis was that I was suffering with a duodonal ulcer that triggered my internal bleeding. Still another test revealed that I had a GIST (gastrointestinal stromal tumor). I went through a nine-hour surgery to remove that tumor.

The Lord was there with me and saw to it that it did not spread. He raised me from my misery and healed my body from this potential fatal calamity. I once again give thanks to God for His healing power. I also praise God for my physician, Dr. Bathel, who operated on me. I am very grateful to him. He was very kind and patient with me. God has given me grace and mercy to endure and manage many health problems.

I was also involved once in a car accident. About fifteen years ago, I was on my way to a prayer meeting in New Kensington. Driving on Route 28 around 6:30 p.m. to my destination, a big tractor trailer left his lane, crossed over to my side of traffic, and crunched my car with two other passengers on board. The Lord spared my life in a miraculous way. His angel was right beside me that day.

There was a paramedic right behind me. He quickly got out of his car and asked me to lie down on the ground along with the other two people who were in the car until the arrival of paramedics truck. They took us to Presbyterian Hospital. After the diagnosis, my right hand and shoulder were fractured, my rotator cuff was damaged, and my right leg had a big deep hole into it. My greatest miracle was that, through it all, I had no pain in my body. My Lord heard my cry and eased all my pain. I praise the Lord for His love and faithfulness, His blessings and kindness toward me.

I grew up and have spent my entire life in the shadows of God's miracles. My mother told me how she was once miraculously healed from a terrible fever. Everyone was worried about her. But one night she said she dreamt about a doctor and a nurse who came to her room and said to her, "You will not die with that disease." Then they gave her a massage with a special oil. In addition, they gave the instruction to prepare a remedy which consisted of grilling black beans and using the powder as coffee. She was to make a drink with it for seven days until she recovered. Following that prescription, my mother was completely healed. God touched my mother's body and restored her through His miraculous working power. The promise He made to Hezekiah centuries earlier that "I will heal you" remains relevant to this very day.

I remember once when I was not feeling well at the orphanage. The shoulder on my right side was aching intensely. At our usual Wednesday night prayer meeting, Mother Dorothy had one of the children call me up for prayer. She said to me the Lord wanted her to pray a special prayer for me. When she did, she put her hand exactly where the pain was. Jesus delivered me from my nagging pain. You see what I mean when I say that divine miracles have followed me every day of my life.

I am also so glad to live in the spirit that "a cheerful heart is good medicine, but a crushed spirit dries up the bones" (Proverbs 17:22). A broken spirit does indeed sap a person's strength. I thank God for keeping me away from the spirit of torment and sadness.

I firmly believe that the joy of the Lord is our strength—and it has certainly been mine. There is a connection between a healthy heart and a positive attitude. It is true that if you would like to stay healthy, you must permanently maintain within you the peace that passes all understanding. Keep yourself from negative thoughts and emotions. Jesus Christ provides the power of prayer, faith, and perseverance so you can achieve this noble objective. He Is always the same and never changes.

I do my best to nurture and enhance my spiritual life by praying, reading the Word every day, and helping others who are in need to the best of my abilities. I am also trying my best to keep the fruits of the Spirit growing in my heart: love, joy, peace, patience, kindness, goodness, faithfulness gentleness, and self-control. I continue to work fervently on the last one, which is self-control.

I praise the Lord my Savior for all these miracles that happened in my lifetime. This attitude of gratitude helps me live with high expectation and hope. Ira F. Stanphill wrote a song with which I identify so very well titled "I Don't Know About Tomorrow."

> *I don't know about tomorrow,*
> *I just live from day to day.*
> *I don't borrow from its sunshine,*
> *For its skies may turn to gray.*
> *I don't worry over the future,*
> *For I know what Jesus said,*
> *And today I'll walk beside Him,*
> *For He knows what is ahead.*

In this life of uncertainties, I make sure I rely every hour on the Lord's power that is always present and at my disposal to help me in time of need.

Chapter 8

BLESSED WITH A WONDERFUL FAMILY

    I have been blessed with a beautiful family of two girls and one boy. They were all born and raised in the city of Pittsburgh where I have spent most of my adult life. Obviously we have put down some deep roots in Pittsburgh.
    Leaving Miami to relocate to Pittsburgh was a process involving a conditioning of my mind and my physical strength. Some of my friends didn't encourage me to come to Pittsburgh because of the climate change. They told me it would be very cold and snowy and that I would not be able to cope with the winter storms. I really had to make up my mind and make the best decision because my husband was already in Pittsburgh. At the end, I too packed my bags and got myself ready for this next chapter in my life with all its changes.
    I relied on God's word to help me make the transition. It is written that "a person's steps are directed by the Lord. How then can

anyone understand their own way?" (Proverbs 20:24). It happened that the day before I got on the plane, there was a forecast for a snow storm for Pittsburgh. I was neither frightened nor worried by this announcement. I had decided to stay calm and let the Lord have His perfect way in my life.

When I arrived I was greeted by a storm, along with Brother Bennie Goodwin and my husband who came to pick me up from the airport. They brought me joy and happiness that far surpassed the bad weather. In fact, I had never known before what snow looked like, so it was somewhat exciting to see it for the first time. The snow was piled high on the ground and it was very windy and cold just as people had warned me. Surprisingly, I liked it because the snow looked so bright and beautiful.

Coming to Pittsburgh was a great blessing for us and our burgeoning family. My arrival was an unforgettable day in my lifetime, in fact a day of victory. I was pregnant with my first child. My husband was attending Pittsburgh Theological Seminary. It was just amazing how God fixed our plan for a victorious new life in the context of a new environment. We were covered with the wings of the angel of the Lord who gave us new family and friends. He took complete control of our needs and wants. What a mighty God we serve!

Bennie Goodwin and his wife Mary were like a brother and sister to us. There was a family from the Mount Lebanon Presbyterian Church that had contacted us at the Seminary. They visited us on different occasions. They picked us up to take us to their house for dinner. They helped me get ready for the coming of the new baby. The Zion Church of God in Christ under Elder Charles Ware and his wife, Sylvia, assisted us in various ways.

The Seminary community was also quite supportive. It was a beautiful campus, a peaceful setting to launch our new adventure. What a wonderful opportunity to discover and adjust to something different in my life. I met new people from different countries. The Seminary staff was great and very helpful. They directed me to a doctor. Thank God for Dr. Bennie Goodwin, our friend and recruiter, who helped my husband enroll at the Pittsburgh Theological Seminary. God is an amazing God. He knew what was the best for us. I want to always be obedient to His calling.

In Pittsburgh, I was also blessed with my happy reunion with Mother who had come from Haiti to live with me. I had to get adjusted living with her all over again because we had been separated from each other for at least twenty-four years. But there is never any mistake in God's amazing grace for us. As my mother moved to be with me in Pittsburgh, she was a great blessing to us. She helped immensely with the children as we had the opportunity and necessity to work.

I had a prediction from an older man in Haiti who told me when I first got pregnant that he had a dream in which he saw me fishing. He interpreted the dream to mean that I will have a baby girl. I was a little bit surprised but then when I went to my doctor for my first visit, he also told me that I would have a beautiful baby girl. This news was a great blessing

Mary Ellen Goodwin

and certainly a confirmation. Since I was clearly anticipating a baby girl, Cindy from the Mount Lebanon Presbyterian Church and her family had a beautiful baby shower for me. Guests kindly brought all kind of things that a baby would have needed, including a bassinet. When the baby was born, we named her Rose Ellen (the Rose is part of my name and Ellen a part of her godmother's name). She was a good baby, and grew into a manageable teen-ager, then a responsible, productive, and respectful young lady.

When my baby was two years old, I found employment in the mail room at the

Pittsburgh Theological Seminary. I had to put her in a daycare facility while I was working. As our friends from the Mount Lebanon Presbyterian Church moved out of Pittsburgh, we lost their contact. The Lord richly blessed us with a new family that cared for us and the good Lord sent us new friends.

A young Jewish lady called us to visit with us. She also had two beautiful children, a baby boy and a little girl. She brought them to play and visit with us. She also had us over her house for dinner at various times. There was a German couple that came as students at the Seminary. The wife's name was Ingrid who also had a baby girl. They were living in our building. We became friends with the family and we enjoyed great fellowship together. Our two little girls played together during the day. The Pittsburgh Theological Seminary had a daycare center where I could leave my child while at work.

Many others in the Pittsburgh community also welcomed us with opened arms. Rodman Street Baptist Church's pastor and his wife, the Reverend and Mrs. George L. Bowick, were always very kind. They made sure we were invited to their house for Thanksgiving dinner. The Reverend Alfred Pugh and his beautiful wife Cleora of the Macedonia Baptist Church always invited us over to their house for dinner as well. Naturally, Bennie and Mary Goodwin and their children helped us tremendously with our baby daughter Rose Ellen. God always took good care of us everywhere we went. We have the lasting testimony that the Lord is always good to my family.

We are well covered by God's free assurance of love and compassion.

My husband used to be a member of the preaching association at Pittsburgh Theological Seminary which gave the students the opportunity to fill temporarily vacant pulpits on different occasions. One Sunday he went preaching to one of those churches in the Butler area. He was driving our very first car in life, a small red Toyota Corolla. That Sunday, my daughter and I did not go with him. He had left early that morning. As it was getting late in the day, he did not show up, so we started to worry about him wondering what could have happened.

We were well relieved when he finally got home around 4:30. It was then that he shared with us how his car turned over upside down on a very slippery road. He related how some people ran over to rescue him from the wreckage of the car. They were able to pull the car from the ravine where it had plunged. He was able to drive the car back to Pittsburgh. The Lord delivered him from this awful accident. On that particular day, we sang for joy and gave thanks for divine protection and restoration.

We spent a good three years at the Pittsburgh Theological Seminary during which we met a lot of loving and kind people. One day I was sick in my apartment and was unable to lift up my arms to take care of my baby who was crying. God sent a neighbor, Bud Pope, who came in, put us in his car, and took me to Presbyterian Hospital. I had then a severe case of bursitis. I considered even this event as God's miracles still shadowing me every step of the way.

I gave birth to our second beautiful little girl, who was happy, jumpy, and jolly. We gave her the name of Françoise Martine after her grandmother. Françoise brought a lot of joy into our lives and sometimes some scary days. One such day happened when, as a baby, I put her in the crib for her nap. After a while, I went to check on her but she was not there. I had looked all over but could not find her. Finally, I checked under the bed, and there she was. It was very scary. Until now I really don't know how she ended up under my bed. Through the Lord's protection, nothing happened to her.

Martine's elementary teacher had a conference with me because she liked to dance in the classroom and was not paying attention. The teacher told me that Martine will never be anything in her life other than a dancer. However, my daughter was a very bright student who has gone through to higher education. I never had to tell her to study or do her homework. Françoise grew up to become a beautiful and responsible young lady who got her college degree and a master's in education. Through her marriage, she has one son, Trevor.

You may ask God by faith whatever you need and He will answer. The psalmist says, "Delight yourself in the Lord, and he will give you the desires of your heart" (Psalm 37:4). Well, the desire of my life was to have a son. I believe my husband was also eager to have a son. God answered our prayers and gave us a son.

I used to babysit a little boy called Charlie. When he sometimes spent the night, I fixed his bed in my room. One time, he was not there, my older daughter Rose Ellen knocked on my door and said, "Mommy, Mommy! I heard a baby crying in your room. Can I help you with Charlie?" I told her that she surely didn't hear any baby crying in my room because Charlie did not come last night.

But the next month I had a dream that my husband was standing at the foot of the bed with a lizard in his hand and the lizard jumped on me. In my dream, I screamed, saying that I was pregnant and it's going to be a boy. Within two months, when I visited my gynecologist, he confirmed that I was pregnant. At my next visit, the ultrasonography test revealed the heartbeat of a baby boy. I praise the Lord for my son who is now married to a nice young lady. They have tree beautiful children.

I am grateful for the beautiful testimonies of love from my two daughters, Rose Ellen and Martine, and son, Frantz. They share here their love and experiences about their mother. Let's begin with Rose Ellen, my first daughter:

Why I Love My Mother

Marie Rozelle Pamphile

My mother was born in Jacmel Haiti to Dr. Abel Gousse and Françoise Marie Joseph. Part of her childhood was spent in an orphanage where she endured many difficult days and nights with little food and a minimal amount of clothing to spare. Her prayers and faith opened doors for her to come to America with a host family that took her in under their watchful care. I am her first child born from her marriage to Leon Pamphile in Pittsburgh, Pennsylvania.

For as long as I can remember, Mother has been an incredible source of strength, courage, and beauty all throughout my life. In fact, I would argue that my mother is a mirror of the virtuous woman found in Proverbs 31. Rozelle is a woman who possesses the virtues of dignity, patience, diligence, generosity, courage, wisdom, and devotion to our God.

The reasons why I love my mother are too numerous to include in one chapter of a book. Her lifetime of devotion to care for me is the reason I am who I am today. Everything, yes everything that she could do for me, she has done and continues to do, with every beat of her heart. As a mother, she has done her very best to raise a young woman using prescribed beauty tips, that I have kept very dearly. In her honor, I would like to share with you several beauty tips that she shared with me. They exemplify why I love my mother, and provide a blueprint for the life she has taught me to live.

Rozelle's Beauty Tips
(Adapted from a poem - author unknown)

- For attractive lips, speak words of kindness.
- For beautiful eyes, love the good in other people.
- To lose weight, let go of stress, hatred, anger, contentment and the need to others.
- To improve your ears, listen to the Word of God.
- Rather than focus on the thorns of life, smell the roses and count your blessing, giving thanks for each one of them.
- For poise, walk with knowledge and self-esteem.
- To strengthen your arms, hug at least three people a day. Touch someone with your love.
- To strengthen your ear, forgive yourself and others.
- Don't worry and hurry so much.

- Rather than walk this earth lightly, walk firmly with determination and leave your mark.
- For the ultimate in business of causal or evening attire, put on the robe of Christ; it fits like a glove but allow room for growth. Best of all, it never goes out of style and is appropriate for any occasion.

Mother has taught me that doing these things on a daily basis will certainly make you a more beautiful person. Why do I love my mother? The reasons are too numerous to recall. Ultimately, I love my mother, because she is the most beautiful glamour girl I know and because she first loved me.

Martine

When I think about my mother, there are so many warm fuzzy feelings and recollections that come mind. She is a hardworking, loving, and caring individual who has sacrificed so much to make sure our family had everything we needed. Without her determination and drive, I myself wouldn't be where I am today. Her story has inspired me to fight in order to make it in a world that is full of so many pitfalls.

My most memorable moments of my mother were that she always made sure that my siblings and I had what we needed. Starting with our hair, which she always took time to make sure it was clean and meticulously styled. Whatever little money she earned, Mom would always purchase clothes and other things. Even as an adult I can say most of the items I have in my house, like pots, pans, and at one point my whole closet, are full of belongings that my mother bought.

If I tell her I'm not feeling well, I know within a few days I could expect a package with some type of vitamins or natural organic herbs to help as a remedy. If it's not one of those things in the box, it will be some type of self-help book. You could pretty much call her a true doctor mom! There is not a book she doesn't have that gives something natural to cure any ailment.

I talk to my mother almost every day. She loves when I call her my baby and she in return calls me her jolly daughter. Just making her laugh and smile makes my day. There is never a conversation that we have where she always reminds me to please read my Bible, especially the book of Proverbs. She always said if there isn't any other book in the Bible to please make sure I read that one.

As a child, I can recall her telling me stories of how she grew up in an orphanage, a life where she would have to pray for food and drink water to fill up her stomach to kill the hunger pains. It was a life where she would pray and wonder when she would ever see her mother again. A life that brought her to a hospital in Port-au-Prince where she found out the nurse attending to her was her half-sister from her father. Can you imagine living a life like this? I can barely make it to lunch without feeling hungry, and once I'm hungry it's hard for me to be productive. I recall her telling me there were times she even blacked out because she was so hungry!

Despite all the hardships Mom faced in

life, she remained a determined and steadfast servant of the Lord. She was dedicated to her and my father's mission to spread God's word through their ministry to help others in Haiti. I can remember seeing her on countless days where she had to prepare thousands of newsletters and envelopes to be mailed to their many supporters. No matter how tired she was, she always fought to help the people of her native land.

    I know that without my mother I wouldn't be where I am today. She has a legacy that I will fight the rest of my life to replicate. Her love and kindness have made her the great woman and mother that she is today, and for that I am forever grateful.

Our Son Frantz

I would like to take a moment to recognize one of the greatest influences in my life, my mom! Most of you know her as Rose, some of you know her has Marie, but to me she will always just be Mom. Since I can remember, she's always been there for me in every way, nurturing me, guiding me, and ensuring that I had everything I needed to succeed. My mother wore many hats. She was a business entrepreneur, a bishop's wife, and the matriarch of the family.

She has instilled the fear of God in me and my sisters to ensure that our lives are filled with patience and wisdom. One of my favorite little nuggets of wisdom that she has given to me goes as follows: "If you are not true to your teeth, they will be false to you!" I have since taken that little bit of knowledge and integrated it into everything I know and do.

Every day that I wake up, I am just so thankful that God has blessed me with such a beautiful, strong, intelligent Mom! Finally, I would just like to say thank you, Mom, for all that you have done and all that you continue to do, I would not be the man I am today without all of your kindness and love.

Conclusion

In this season of my life, I wholeheartedly praise the Lord for enabling me to daily walk in the shadow of His miracles. As I look back on the tough years of my childhood and youth, I realize that I have truly come this far by faith, leaning on the Lord. I am grateful for His unfailing love.

I am grateful to my mother who gave me birth. She was a child of God who dedicated her life to unselfish service. Though she was not able to meet my needs, she was always concerned about giving me the best education and upbringing possible under our circumstances. That was the reason she placed me in an orphanage.

I am very grateful to the founder of the Church of God in Christ and to Mother Dorothy W. Exume. Mother Dorothy was in her twenties when she went to Haiti with Bishop C. H. Mason's approval to serve as a missionary in the first foreign mission outpost of the Church of God in Christ. While in Haiti, she founded the orphanage where I spent nine years of my life. Through the ups and downs and the vicissitudes of life, Mother Exumé managed to take care of a group of twenty girls. She also had high aspirations for us. She wanted us to become saved and productive citizens of society. I was so blessed to experience God's miraculous deeds under her graceful tutelage.

I also thank God for the Pittsburgh Theological Seminary that was there for my husband and me. My husband received a very good theological education that has helped him to help others. I am grateful for all the friends we met there and the support they gave us in our life journey.

I am forever thankful for all the miraculous events that had overshadowed me throughout my life. In the course of my life's trajectory, God has always connected me with people who were nice and supportive to me. I count it all joy and I continue to express gratitude for the blessings of the Lord.

Let me conclude with the words of Helen Steiner Rice who translate so well the abiding presence and unfailing love of God in my life:

... On the earth and in the sky,
HE'S EVER PRESENT and ALWAYS THERE
To take you in His tender care
And bind the wounds and mend the breaks
When all the world around forsakes ...
SOMEONE CARES
AND LOVES YOU STILL
AND GOD IS THE SOMEONE
who always will.

- Helen Steiner Rice

Biography of Rozelle Pamphile

Marie-Rozelle Pamphile is a native of Haiti. She relocated to the United States in March 1968. She resided in Florida for two years before moving to the Pittsburgh area over five decades ago. She has been married to her teenaged year's sweetheart Leon Pamphile. They have been blessed with a beautiful family of three children and now six grandchildren..

Mrs. Pamphile attended public schools in Haiti. Upon coming to Bradenton, FL., she continued her studies in the Manatee County Schools to receive her high school diploma in 1969. Upon arriving in Pittsburgh, she attended the Community college of Allegheny County. She worked for seven years as a printer and adressographer at the Matthias Printing Company downtown Pittsburgh.

In later years, she enrolled at the Pittsburgh Beauty Academy that awarded her a diploma as a Cosmetology Teacher in 1984. She completed these studies at the University of Pittsburgh where she received a Professional

Certificate in Cosmetology entitling her to teach in the schools of the Commonwealth of Pennsylvania in 1984. Mrs. Pamphile enjoyed a successful career as a cosmetologist in Pittsburgh.

She has dedicated herself to a lifelong career of service to the Lord and to humanity. She is the co-founder of the Functional Literacy Ministry, (FLM-Haiti), a 501(c3) organization established in Pittsburgh in 1983. FLM-Haiti provides, through Christ, education, health care and hope to the people of Haiti. She has immensely contributed to the growth of the organization that in average operates 70 literacy centers, a K-13 school, the House of David Health Care Center, and the Excelsior Technical Institute. Since 2011, she has been living as the Associate Executive Director of FLM-Haiti.

Lady Pamphile had closely worked with her husband in ministry in New Kensington as they pastored the First Church of God there for eighteen years. During that time, she sang in in the choir and faithfully served as Superintendent of Sunday School. She was such a great encourager to the whole congregation and especially sensitive to the ministry to children and youth.

Lady. Pamphile is actively involved with the Haitian community in Pittsburgh. She is very sensitive to the needs of the hopeless and helpless. She helps Haitians here to find jobs and housing. She is an interpreter for the Haitians for the Pittsburgh Board of Education. She also served as President of the International Women in the Pittsburgh/Monroeville/Murrysville areas.

Since 2011, she became the First Lady of the Church of God in Christ Jurisdiction of Haiti. She is working along her husband who was appointed Bishop of that Jurisdiction. As First Lady, she is supporting the Women Department. She is especially interested in the orphanage where she herself resided for many years. She served as an active participant in the Church's reconstruction effort since the 2010 earthquake and in the great endeavor to rebuild lives.

www.ingramcontent.com/pod-product-compliance
Lightning Source LLC
LaVergne TN
LVHW021600070426
835507LV00014B/1872